EAT LIKE A LOCAL BOOK SERIES

Eat Like a Local- Sarasota: Sarasota Florida Food Guide

I have lived in the Sarasota area since 1998 and learned about many great places that I want to try. –Conoal

EAT LIKE A LOCAL-CONNECTICUT: Connecticut Food Guide

This a great guide to try different places in Connecticut to eat. Can't wait to try them all! The author is awesome to explore and try all these different foods/drinks. There are places I didn't know they existed until I got this book and I am a CT resident myself! –Caroline J. H.

EAT LIKE A LOCAL- LAS VEGAS: Las Vegas Nevada Food Guide

Perfect food guide for any tourist traveling to Vegas or any local looking to go outside their comfort zone! –TheBondes

Eat Like a Local-Jacksonville: Jacksonville Florida Food Guide

Loved the recommendations. Great book from someone who knows their way around Jacksonville. –Anonymous

EAT LIKE A LOCAL- COSTA BRAVA: Costa Brava Spain Food Guide

The book was very well written. Visited a few of the restaurants in the book, they were great! Sylvia V.

Eat Like a Local-Sacramento: Sacramento California Food Guide

As a native of Sacramento, Emerald's book touches on some of our areas premier spots for food and fun. She skims the surface of what Sacramento has to offer recommending locations in historical, popular areas where even more jewels can be found. –Katherine G.

EAT LIKE A LOCAL- SOUTH CAROLINA

South Carolina Food Guide

Kelly Dawn Jurgensen

Eat Like a Local-South Carolina Copyright © 2021 by CZYK Publishing LLC. All Rights Reserved.

All rights reserved. No part of this book may be reproduced in any form or by any electronic or mechanical means including information storage and retrieval systems, without permission in writing from the author. The only exception is by a reviewer, who may quote short excerpts in a review.

The statements in this book are of the authors and may not be the views of CZYK Publishing.

Cover designed by: Lisa Rusczyk Ed. D.

CZYK Publishing Since 2011.
CZYKPublishing.com
Eat Like a Local

Lock Haven, PA
All rights reserved.
ISBN: 9798491787609

BOOK DESCRIPTION

Are you excited about planning your next trip? Do you want an edible experience? Would you like some culinary guidance from a local? If you answered yes to any of these questions, then this Eat Like a Local book is for you. Eat Like a Local – South Carolina by author Kelly Dawn Jurgensen offers the inside scoop on food in South Carolina. It is heavy on country cooking. She's been to Oklahoma, Georgia, Florida, and up the east coast. Nothing compares, however, to the comfort of country food. Culinary tourism is an important aspect of any travel experience. Food has the ability to tell you a story of a destination, its landscapes, and culture on a single plate. Most food guides tell you how to eat like a tourist. Although there is nothing wrong with that, as part of the Eat Like a Local series, this book will give you a food guide from someone who has lived at your next culinary destination.

In these pages, you will discover advice on having a unique edible experience. This book will not tell you exact addresses or hours but instead will give you excitement and knowledge of food and drinks from a local that you may not find in other travel food guides.

Eat like a local. Slow down, stay in one place, and get to know the food, people, and culture. By the time you finish this book, you will be eager and prepared to travel to your next culinary destination.

OUR STORY

Traveling has always been a passion of the creator of the Eat Like a Local book series. During Lisa's travels in Malta, instead of tasting what the city offered, she ate at a large fast-food chain. However, she realized that her traveling experience would have been more fulfilling if she had experienced the best of local cuisines. Most would agree that food is one of the most important aspects of a culture. Through her travels, Lisa learned how much locals had to share with tourists, especially about food. Lisa created the Eat Like a Local book series to help connect people with locals which she discovered is a topic that locals are very passionate about sharing. So please join me and: Eat, drink, and explore like a local.

TABLE OF CONTENTS

Eat Like a Local-
Book Series Reviews
BOOK DESCRIPTION
OUR STORY
TABLE OF CONTENTS
DEDICATION
ABOUT THE AUTHOR
HOW TO USE THIS BOOK
FROM THE PUBLISHER
1. How Do You Take Your Barbeque?
2. Sweet Tea: The Champagne Of The South
3. Boiled Peanuts: Caviar Of The South
4. Peaches: The Official State Fruit
5. Biscuits, Like Grandma Used To Make, And The History
6. Pecans (We pronounce it pea-CAN in these parts)
7. Grits (That's What You Call Them)
8. Collard Greens: Official South Carolina State Vegetable
9. Okra: Slimy, But Satisfying (Yes, I kind of paraphrased The Lion King)
10. Pimento Cheese: Its Own Food Group
11. Chicken Bog
12. Macaroni and Cheese: No, not Kraft!

13. Cornbread: How Do You Like Yours?
14. Frogmore Stew: No Frogs Were Harmed, We Promise.
15. Fried Seafood (We Deep Fry Almost Everything!)
16. Meat 'n Three
17. Blenheim Ginger Ale
18. Sweet Potatoes (And A Shut My Mouth)
19. Chow Chow
20. Duke's Mayonnaise
21. Fried Chicken
22. Hot Sauce (We DO Put That S#&* On Everything)
23. Desserts
24. Upscale Establishments (Yes, We Can Be Fancy Too!)

Bonus Tips

Other Resources:

READ OTHER BOOKS BY CZYK PUBLISHING

DEDICATION

This book is dedicated to Paul, Sarah, Rachel, and Connor. I'd also like to make a dedication to my mom, Sandra and grandma, Mertie. Without the recipes and experience cooking handed down from them, this book might not have been possible. I can't fail to mention my sister, Jessica. I love you all!

ABOUT THE AUTHOR

Dawn is a native South Carolinian who lives with her husband, two daughters, and son. She lives in a small town approximately 45 minutes from the capital of Columbia. Kelly loves to read and attend rock concerts. She is a huge fan of Def Leppard. She also loves 80s hair bands and goes to at least 5 concerts a year. Once a year, she and her husband, Paul, go on a cruise called the Monsters of Rock Cruise. It' s nonstop concerts and it's a great time. It's the only time of year that she eats anything but country cooking and tries food from around the world.

Before she started writing, Kelly got a bachelor's degree in Management and English from the University of South Carolina. After that, she worked as a computer technician for 10 years. She then was given the opportunity to return to school full time to pursue a career as a surgical technologist. 8 years later, she realized that she wanted to learn more, so she started school as a surgical first assistant. She wanted to be able to not only help with someone's surgery, but also to suture them closed. She has grown up on country cooking, with recipes passed down through the generations.

HOW TO USE THIS BOOK

The goal of this book is to help culinary travelers either dream or experience different edible experiences by providing opinions from a local. The author has made suggestions based on their own knowledge. Please do your own research before traveling to the area in case the suggested locations are unavailable.

Travel Advisories: As a first step in planning any trip abroad, check the Travel Advisories for your intended destination.
https://travel.state.gov/content/travel/en/traveladvisories/traveladvisories.html

FROM THE PUBLISHER

Traveling can be one of the most important parts of a person's life. The anticipation and memories that you have are some of the best. As a publisher of the *Eat Like a Local*, Greater Than a Tourist, as well as the popular *50 Things to Know* book series, we strive to help you learn about new places, spark your imagination, and inspire you. Wherever you are and whatever you do I wish you safe, fun, and inspiring travel.

Lisa Rusczyk Ed. D.
CZYK Publishing

Eat Like a Local

"I am not a glutton. I am an explorer of food."

~ Erma Bombeck

South Carolina is a melting pot of cultures. It has strong roots going back to 1670 when it was by the English. South Carolina became the eighth state to ratify the U.S. constitution in 1788. Its early economy was largely agricultural, benefitting from fertile soil, and plantation farmers relied on the slave trade for cheap labor to maximize their profits. By 1730, people of African descent made up two thirds of the colony's population. South Carolina became the first state to secede from the union in 1861 and was the site of the first shots of the Civil War. Today, the South Carolina coast is looked to as a sunny vacation getaway for not only locals, but people from all over the country. Famous South Carolinians include musicians James Brown, Chubby Checker and Dizzy Gillespie, novelist Pat Conroy, boxer Joe Frazier, tennis champion Althea Gibson, politician Jesse Jackson, and country singer Lee Brice, and Hootie and the Blowfish, to name a few. South Carolina has a rich history born of necessity and ingenuity. Its dishes have been passed down through generations. If you have a hankering for barbeque, shrimp and grits, or just plain old comfort food, South Carolina has a ton of not only old-fashioned foods, but drinks as well. We love our sweet tea here. The sweeter the better.

> *"In my south, the most treasured things passed down from generation to generation are the family recipes."*
>
> ~ Robert St. John

Eat Like a Local

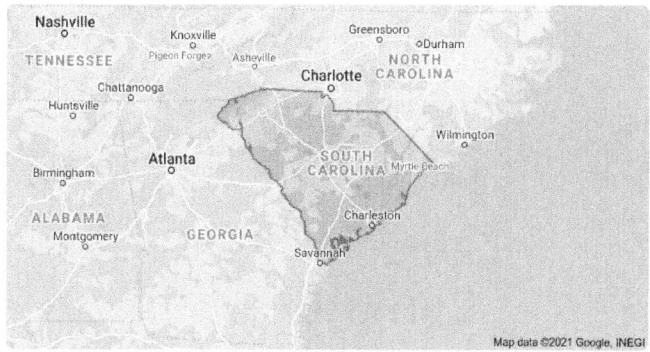

South Carolina
United States

Columbia South Carolina Climate

	High	Low
January	58	36
February	63	39
March	71	46
April	80	53
May	86	62
June	92	69
July	95	72
August	93	71
September	88	66
October	78	54
November	69	45
December	61	39

GreaterThanaTourist.com

Temperatures are in Fahrenheit degrees.
Source: NOAA

1. HOW DO YOU TAKE YOUR BARBEQUE?

"What we can confidently boast, though, is that the Palmetto State has one of the country's oldest and most vibrant barbecue traditions. In fact, the form of whole-hog cooking practiced in the Pee Dee region is the closest approximation to the way barbecue was cooked back in the colonial and antebellum days."

~ Robert F. Moss

Here in South Carolina, we take our barbeque seriously. There is an ongoing debate as to what base is the best. Some prefer vinegar base, some prefer tomato base, and others mustard base. I am of the high opinion that a vinegar-based sauce is the best. It's tangy without being overwhelming. It gets you right by the ear with a twinge. The vinegar sauce can be used with beef, chicken, or pork. Where I am from, however, we use it for pork. Roasting long and slow over a wood burning pit while periodically basting gives so much flavor!

If you find your way to Manning, which is my hometown, D&H Bar-B-Que is the hands down favorite. D&H has been locally owned since 1947 by the Brailsford family. The site was originally a fast-food drive-in. They're all-you-can-eat buffet has so many choices. D&H Bar-B-Que specializes in homemade barbeque, fried chicken, fried pork chops, hash and rice, and best of all, homemade mac and cheese.

They offer a secret homemade sauce recipe that they make fresh every day. D&H offers the "Williamsburg County" style of BBQ doused with a vinegar-based sauce, unlike the standard mustard-based BBQ which is very popular in South Carolina. The hash, yet another SC BBQ staple and an original to the state, is a bit different but quite tasty. D&H Bar-B-Que always serves fresh vegetables, coleslaw, and potato salad. Don't forget the hush puppies, those delicious little nuggets of deep-fried cornbread

Eat Like a Local

heaven. D&H also has, if you're so inclined, fried pig skins. They are so good!

Stop in on seafood night, which is on Tuesday and Saturday nights. D&H serves catfish nuggets, catfish stew, and some of the largest fried shrimp you've ever seen. Make sure you save room for dessert at this place, the pecan pie is fantastic!

If you're a mustard-based barbeque lover, like any good origin story, there is some controversy: Did the Bessinger family come up with the recipe or did the Sweatmans first create it? No way to ever be sure, but all signs point to Orangeburg County, SC, as being its likely birthplace. Both the Bessingers and Sweatman's hail from the Holly Hill area of the county.

The Sweatmans

Mr. and Mrs. Harold Sweatman (Bub and Margie) in 1959 opened a small barbeque place in the town of Holly Hill, SC. They then closed and only cooked for special gatherings with family and friends. Cooking for these occasions took place in the "old dairy" which was located just a few yards from the Sweatman's home. They didn't open

a barbeque restaurant until 1977.

The bar-b-que was and continues to be cooked fresh every week. Oak, hickory, and pecan trees are cut and split for the wood that is burned in the cooking process. They have pulled pork, ribs, and chicken. Sides choices include hash and rice, cole slaw, baked beans, green beans, mac & cheese, and banana pudding. Pork Skins are automatically included for free on all pork plates until they are gone. They are open Friday-Saturday.

The Bessingers

The Bessinger family refers to themselves as the "first family of barbeque in South Carolina." They are known for their legendary mustard-based barbeque sauce, around since the 1930s. They have kept the business in the family ever since. Bessingers Barbeque is located in Charleston and open Monday-

Sunday. They offer such choices as brisket, burgers, turkey, and incredible sides of potato salad, steak fries, baked beans, green beans, hash and rice, coleslaw, pork skins, okra, collard greens, mac and cheese, and onion rings. Save room for dessert, because they have banana pudding, peanut butter pie, Oreo cheesecake, and pecan pie.

If you're partial to tomato-based barbeque, then look no further than Bucky's BBQ in Greenville. Bucky's BBQ is a local and family-owned BBQ restaurant in Greenville, South Carolina, and is known for its wood smoked flavor. Bucky's has pulled pork, chicken and ribs. Sides include green beans, baked beans, Cajun pinto beans, mac and cheese, potato salad, Cole slaw, and cucumber, tomato, and onion salad. They offer desserts such as chocolate chip cookies, banana pudding, and a divine sweet potato crunch.

Regardless of your sauce preference, there are tons of options available all over the state of South

Carolina. All you have to do is bring your stretchy pants and your appetite.

2. SWEET TEA: THE CHAMPAGNE OF THE SOUTH

There's a southern saying that says, "here in the South, We don't hide crazy. We parade it around on the front porch and give it sweet tea." Sweet tea is synonymous with the south. We don't measure the sugar; we just know how much sugar goes into it. There are many variations, from peach, to lemon to raspberry. Some people add lemonade. Most people, however, just take it straight. There is nothing like a cold glass of sweet tea on a hot day.

20 miles south of Charleston, South Carolina on Wadmalaw Island resides the only tea plantation in the United States. It is special to my family, because my Uncle Mack Fleming purchased the company from the Lipton Company in 1987 with his partner, Bill Barclay-Hall. I remember every year at family

reunions, Uncle Mack would bring his tea. At the time, it was called American Classic Tea. The Charleston Tea Garden is open to visitors for free and gives tours as well as tastings.

3. BOILED PEANUTS: CAVIAR OF THE SOUTH

Boiled peanuts are a snack staple in the south and some people consider it a delicacy. They are the official state snack of South Carolina. Boiled peanuts can be found anywhere from roadside stands to gas stations to festivals. Bluffton boasts of a boiled peanut festival every year. There is a peanut cookoff, a peanut spitting contest (yes, gross, but I guess some people think it's fun), and live music. You can even get your picture taken with the world's largest boiled peanut. It measures 22 feet long, weighs nearly a half-ton, and is a one-of-a-kind plywood-and-spray-foam sight. It was built by Jared Jester, Clayton Colleran, and Hannah Parrish for the Boiled Peanut Festival in

2013. This large nut once stood at South of the Border until it was purchased by Cahill's Market in 2014. It is now the focal point of the festival.

Peanuts are also called Goober Peas, named from a Civil War folk song. Peanuts were brought to America by slaves. Stories passed down through generations say that soldiers didn't have access to bread, so they ate what they could. Peanuts were easy to transport. Boiled peanuts are an acquired taste. Some people can't get past the juice or slickness of the peanut when the shell is opened. Others just love slurping the juice and the softness of the peanut. Many people love enjoying the boiled peanuts with an iced cold Coke. So, if you're driving the back roads or even Interstates of South Carolina, you're bound to come across a sign for this snack. Try 'em. You just might like 'em.

4. PEACHES: THE OFFICIAL STATE FRUIT

"An apple is an excellent thing -
- until you have tried a peach."

~ George du Maurier

Also called the Persian apple, the peach tree was first cultivated in the North-Western region of China near the Kunlun Mountains around 6000 BC and soon spread throughout the world. The peach tree (Prunus persica) is a deciduous fruit tree that is native to China. It was first transported to the West by the Persians and then by the Romans.

The most important peach-producing regions in the Northern hemisphere are the United States (California, South Carolina, Colorado, Georgia) and the neighboring regions of Canada. The peach contains vitamins A, C, B1, B2, B6, and minerals such as potassium, phosphorus, magnesium, calcium, sulfur, chlorine, manganese, copper and iron. Peaches are considered as a symbol of longevity and good luck. It is considered one of the 20 essential foods for a healthy life.

In some Latin American countries, it is known by the name durazno and is very popular there. There are over 200 varieties of peaches.

Peaches and apricots are very similar. The only thing that separates them is a gene. The average peach tree can live up to 12 years. A peach tree can grow up to 33 feet tall.

The term "you are a peach" has a story to it. There once was a tradition where people gave peaches to their friends that they liked the most. Peaches in literature can be traced back to the year 79 AD. However, some people claim that peaches were first mentioned in Chinese writings in the time around 10 BC.

China is still the largest producer of Peaches in the world. But in the U.S., Contrary to public knowledge, South Carolina comes in second to California in peach production. When you talk about peaches, most people think of Georgia. South Carolina, however, produces more! Aiken, South Carolina is home to peach farms. With that peach production comes boundless recipes. A very popular dish made with peaches is cobbler. It's ooey, gooey sweetness. While cobbler is made all over the state, Peaches 'n' Such in Monetta has the best peach cobbler. Peaches 'N' Such started as a roadside stand in the 90's and has since grown into a small retail store where you can grab breakfast, lunch and dinner. You can buy the produce harvested directly from the fields, or you can enjoy them at a nice sit-down area. They have farm-to-table options each day. Surrounded by orchards, it offers peach cobbler, peach tea, peach ice cream, pickled peaches, peach preserves, and even cider.

It has been said that the best eateries are found on roadsides and far off the beaten path and Peaches 'n' Such lives up to the name. They are open in summer Monday-Sunday.

5. BISCUITS, LIKE GRANDMA USED TO MAKE, AND THE HISTORY

"All the fast-food places sell biscuits these days and they advertise them 'just like your mother made.' I don't like for anybody to insult my mother that way."

~ Lewis Grizzard

The word biscuit comes from the Latin word panis biscoctus, which means twice baked. Soldiers in ancient Rome received "hard biscuits" in their rations that had no leavening agent or fat, so they lasted a long time. Hard biscuits have been around for centuries, and they were also called hardtack, ship's biscuit, sea biscuit and pilot bread.

The recipes of biscuits we eat these days in the U.S. haven't been around very long. History hasn't always documented biscuits as being at the center of hearty breakfasts or chicken dinners. They were hard, thin, durable, dry and a necessity, not a luxury.

Even in the antebellum days, biscuits were still tough and flat, and usually were only eaten in wealthy homes. Most people living in the South at the time ate cornbread instead. That's because most mills in the South were great at grinding corn but not at processing wheat. So only the rich could afford flour, which often had to be shipped in from northern states.

Beaten biscuits were a bit of a step up from hardtack and were the next evolution to what we have today. They included fat like butter or lard, but still no leavening agent, so beaten biscuits remained flat and only slightly lighter because the dough required 15 minutes of kneading or beating.

It wasn't until several 19th-century innovations came along that we got what's now recognized as a Southern biscuit. Better flour mills increased wheat production which dropped the price of flour enough that poor Southerners could also afford to buy flour. The development of chemical leavening agents, such as pearl ash (potassium carbonate), potassium bicarbonate, and sodium bicarbonate (baking soda) helped elevate biscuits without yeast or beaten eggs.

Southerners love biscuits. Those buttery, scratch-made, flaky morsels of goodness go right to the heart of South Carolina. We can eat them with every meal. Biscuit recipes vary and can be made with lard or buttermilk. They can be made to go with sweet or even savory items. Growing up, we ate biscuits and syrup. My grandma and mom growing up made them with Crisco and buttermilk. I remember not being able to wait for them to even cool and ate them fresh out of the oven. Biscuits can be found on menus in restaurants across South Carolina. They are brought out like bread is at most restaurants. One special place is Callie's Hot Little Biscuit in Charleston. They have so many options that they even have a sampler platter. So, if you have a hankering for that buttery, flaky, goodness, give Callie's a try. One final fun fact, after the Civil War, early blues singers used food as metaphors for sex. The word "biscuit" described an attractive woman, and the term "biscuit roller" described a woman who was good in bed.

6. PECANS (WE PRONOUNCE IT PEA-CAN IN THESE PARTS)

"Pecans are not cheap, my hons. In fact, in the South, the street value of shelled pecans just before holiday baking season is roughly that of crack cocaine. Do not confuse the two. It is almost impossible to make a decent crack cocaine tassie, I am told."

~ Celia Rivenbark

The name "pecan" comes from the Algonquian word, paccan, which roughly translates as "nut requiring a stone to crack." Some people say "pea-CAN" and others, "pea-KAHN." No matter how you pronounce it (we won't hold it against you), these sweet and buttery flavored nuts are good straight out of the shell and even better in a pecan pie. Pecans come from a tree; a species of hickory dubbed Carya illinoinensis. South Carolina has the perfect weather for growing pecans. Trees can produce for 300 years or more.

The wood from pecan trees is also beneficial. The trees can grow over 150 feet tall. It can be used in carpentry and the oil for cosmetics.

It takes three years for a tree to mature enough to produce fruit. A healthy 10- to 12-year-old specimen can yield some 600 pounds of nuts per year.

Early Native Americans ate pecan nutmeats and also ground them into a sweet, creamy liquid called hickory milk, which they used to thicken broths and season hominy and other foods. Wild pecans have been esteemed since colonial times, and homesteads and plantations had groves of the trees, but the nuts weren't grown commercially until the late 1800s. In the early 20th century, Boone Hall Plantation had the largest pecan grove in the country. There are more than 500 varieties. Today, pecans are a multimillion-dollar crop in South Carolina. South Carolina isn't the highest producer of pecans, however. We still like them a lot. They are easy to crack and have been used in Lowcountry cooking for pies, cobblers, and

Eat Like a Local

candies like pralines and pecan brittle. They are even used as topping for sweet potato casseroles, which grace the tables at Thanksgiving.

Pecans aren't just used in desserts, however. Many restaurants use it to crust fish. They are an excellent source of vitamins, protein, and unsaturated fats. Recent clinical research has found that eating about a handful of them each day may help lower cholesterol levels and delay age-related muscle and nerve degeneration.

In Florence, Young Plantations Pecans has got it going on. They have so many options for enjoying pecans. They have them in sweet and heat. So, if you're a pecan lover, Young Plantations Pecans is a treat. They are open Monday- Sunday.

7. GRITS (THAT'S WHAT YOU CALL THEM)

"What is a Grit?"

~ Vincent Gambino My Cousin Vinny

Grits are made from grinding corn into a course meal. Grits can be found on breakfast menus across the state. Mr. Tipton in My Cousin Vinny was right when he said "No self-respecting southerner uses instant grits. I take pride in my grits." It does take 20 minutes to cook grits to perfection. Grits has also made its way into a 1980's sitcom, Alice. The phrase "Mel, kiss my grits" was spoken by Flo almost every episode. While it has nothing to do with actual grits, it's still a cute mention of a food that is so popular here. Grits don't have a strong taste at all, even though many people who haven't tried them think that they will taste like the corn they are made from. Grits take on and are enhanced by additions to it.

They have increased in popularity with the addition of shrimp. Sauteed shrimp, grits, melted butter, salt, and pepper make up the basic recipe. Of course, there are variations. With the ports of Charleston being so close by, South Carolinians have the opportunity to get fresh shrimp to go with their grits. One popular place to get your grits is Poogan's Porch. Poogan's Porch is Charleston's oldest eating establishment and was opened in 1976. It is located in a restored Victorian house and offers brunch and dinner. Poogan's has a dish called Sunrise Shrimp & Grits, which is amped up with a ham gravy, peppers, onions, and sausage. Poogan's shrimp and grits is slap your momma good! They are open Monday – Sunday.

8. COLLARD GREENS: OFFICIAL SOUTH CAROLINA STATE VEGETABLE

When it comes to southern cooking, it's often the side dish that takes the center stage. In South Carolina, a heaping side of collard greens fits the bill. One of the most popular complements to any South Carolina meal, collard greens are a staple of the Palmetto State's cuisine and were named the official state vegetable in 2011. Just how did these leafy vegetables become such a prominent part of South Carolina's cuisine? It all boils down to how they were prepared. While collard greens were already being grown in the Southern colonies, they didn't gain popularity until the African slaves began preparing them in their own unique way. This method consisted of cooking the greens in a liquid called pot likker, a stock usually made up of chicken broth, onion, salt, pepper or pepper flakes and a smoky ham hock. This flavor-rich stock is what transformed collard greens

Eat Like a Local

from simple, leafy greens into a cherished South Carolina tradition. Visitors of South Carolina often overlook this leafy delight at first glance, opting for something which sounds more appetizing than a side of vegetables. But if they're lucky, a friendly local will steer them in the right direction. Aside from being uniquely delicious, collard greens also boast several health benefits. They're rich in vitamins and calcium, help lower cholesterol and reduce the risk of cancer. Collards can be found on just about every menu in country cooking restaurants. They're usually cooked with ham hocks. Ham hocks are also known as pork knuckles. They come from the bottom of the pork leg, and they're mostly bone, fat, connective tissue, and some meat. One restaurant to try in Sumter (my current home) is Jeffrey Lampkin's Country Boy Kitchen. Opened in 2019 by American Idol Finalist Jeffrey Lampkin, CBK is the Lord's soul food. They not only have a restaurant in Sumter, but also a food truck that travels to surrounding towns. They also opened another restaurant in Bishopville in August 2021. CBK offers such sides as Soul Saving greens (collards), Yaweah Yams (sweet potatoes), Good God Almighty Green Beans, and Rice and Glory (Gravy) to name a few. It's so popular, that you can even make reservations!

9. OKRA: SLIMY, BUT SATISFYING (YES, I KIND OF PARAPHRASED THE LION KING)

Stewed or fried, okra is so good. Okra, or more formally Abelmoschus esculentus Moench, is a popular ingredient in Southern cuisine. Okra is a member of the cotton and hibiscus families. Its origin is disputed with West Africa, Ethiopia and South Asia, as the plant itself thrives in tropical and subtropical regions around the world and is highly tolerant to heat and drought. The pod is first mentioned as a food staple in an account from 1216 by a Spanish Moor visiting Egypt. From there, okra spread through the Mediterranean and eventually came to the Americas via the Atlantic slave trade in

Eat Like a Local

the late 1650s. It has become a beloved addition to the Southern table in all forms: fried, roasted, boiled (as a thickener for soups and gumbo), dried, steamed, pickled and even thinly sliced and eaten raw. Okra can be grown in all soil types.

Don't let the okra "goo" turn you off from trying it. They can be used in stir fry's and adding some acid to it balances it out. Okra is also very good in gumbo and vegetable soup. The leaves can be used in salads and be sautéed like greens. Okra seeds can be roasted and ground for a caffeine-free substitute for coffee.

Page's Okra Grill in Mount Pleasant is one of many restaurants in South Carolina to try stewed okra and tomatoes. Page's Okra Grill combines simple dishes with traditional coastal seafood. Their focus is on using fresh, seasonal, and local ingredients whenever available. They are open Saturday – Monday.

10. PIMENTO CHEESE: ITS OWN FOOD GROUP

"I've never met a problem that cheese couldn't solve."

~ A Wise Guy

Out of all the iconic foods in the South, pimento cheese is one of the most famous. The earliest mention is a recipe found in a 1912 Columbia fundraising cookbook. Pimento cheese is a spread and a dip. Growing up, I remember it being present at every potluck and even weddings, either in a dip or on small finger sandwiches. I love it on a sandwich and also to dip my pita chips in for a snack. Many people not from the south have no idea what pimento cheese is. Some people call it southern pate. No matter how famous it is in the south, it actually came from New York! I'm sure finding this information out has many die-hard southerners clutching their pearls and in vapors (just kidding, it's not that bad).

Pimento cheese is made up of mayonnaise, shredded cheddar cheese and diced pimientos. Pimentos are a type of pepper with a sweet flavor and very little heat. This nightshade is also known as a cherry pepper because of its red color and round, heart-shaped fruit. They usually measure about 3 to 4 inches long and 2 to 3 inches wide, with a short, thick green stem. A lot of people know pimentos by the little orange thing stuffed into olives. Pimento cheese can be served hot or cold and can be found in local grocery stores under the Palmetto Cheese brand name. The recipe originated with Sassy Henry. Sassy, her husband Brian, and their two children moved to Pawleys Island, SC in 2002 where they took over the historic Sea View Inn. Palmetto Cheese was first introduced in local market outlets in Pawleys Island and Georgetown, SC in 2006. During visits to the Lowcountry, tourists would purchase Palmetto Cheese to take home. Palmetto Cheese is available to ship nationwide.

11. CHICKEN BOG

Chicken bog is a delicious chicken, rice and sausage dish, and it's very much a South Carolina thing. Folks in surrounding states are likely to give you a blank stare if you mention it. It's closely related to chicken pilau (or pilaf or perlo), except that it's thicker. It's moister than chicken perlo, which is more common in Georgetown County, just to the south of Horry County.

We love our rice in South Carolina. Chicken bog is simple, quick to make, and can feed a crowd, making it a great addition to potlucks and family reunions. Throughout the 1700s until the Civil War, South Carolina was the largest rice producer in the nation, but it wasn't grown commercially through the 1900s. In recent years, Carolina Plantation Rice in Darlington and Anson Mills, based in Columbia, have begun growing rice again.

The capital of the chicken bog world is Loris, where they've been saluting this favorite dish at the Loris Bog-Off Festival since 1979.

Outside of home kitchens and potlucks, chicken bog is hard to find. One dish close to chicken bog is Turkey Prioleau, which can be found at Bertha's Kitchen in Charleston. Bertha's Kitchen was opened in 1979. Bertha's is inexpensive and informal, but every meal is prepared to order. Bertha's is open every day.

12. MACARONI AND CHEESE: NO, NOT KRAFT!

"All I want…is mac and cheese."

~ Kurt Cobain

I'm a sucker for a good mac and cheese. We southerners know our mac and cheese. It's a little-known fact that Thomas Jefferson helped introduce Americans to the humble mac and cheese. Before then, however, the first pasta-and-cheese recipes were written in Italy in the 1300s. For a long time, only the rich could afford it and it was considered a delicacy.

By the 1930s, cooks in the U.S. were preparing it with cheap American cheddar and noodles instead of expensive parmesan and pasta imported from Italy. During the Great Depression, many people were struggling to feed their families. It wasn't until a pasta salesman in St. Louis, Missouri came up with the idea to sell his macaroni pasta noodles with a packet of processed cheese. They were called meal kits and became a very popular way for families to eat and not spend a lot of money. Who would have thought that something that had such lofty beginnings would become so humble?

These days, you can't go to a family reunion or potluck without seeing an abundance of mac and cheese casserole dishes. Mac and cheese should be gooey and so good it'll make you want to slap your momma. I have seen some people try to "jazz up" a recipe by adding corn. This is a sacrilege and is uncalled for! Mac and cheese is not to be messed with or messed up. You can find it on any southern cuisine-based restaurant menu across the state.

13. CORNBREAD: HOW DO YOU LIKE YOURS?

Every time I think about cornbread, I think about the movie, Life, starring Eddie Murphy and Martin Lawrence. When one of the prisoners asks the question "you goin' eat your cornbread?" This starts a rant by Eddie's character. It's hilarious! "You can't have my cornbread. That's for damn sure. Cause if you try and take my cornbread, Part 2 of my killing spree is gon' begin up in here on your ass, right now. You thinking about my cornbread, better get the taste out your mouth. That's for damn sure."

We Southerners are serious about our cornbread. Many argue that it should be sweet. Others

Eat Like a Local

that no sugar be allowed anywhere near the cornmeal. I am of the opinion that it should not be sweet. Cornbread has always been a Southern staple due to the high availability of corn among Southern crops. Corn grows well in the heat and humidity of the South. We are known for our biscuits, but they weren't as common in earlier times.

Cornbread began as corn pone: cornmeal, water, and a dash of salt. The addition of milk (usually buttermilk) and eggs makes it cornbread. Cornbread is traditionally cooked in a cast iron skillet.

Cornbread can be found on menus of just about any restaurant in South Carolina that serves traditional southern food. It has even found a cult following in the form of fried hush puppies. A variation of cornbread is to add sharp cheddar cheese and jalapenos. you take your cornbread, it's definitely a filling accompaniment to a great meal.

14. FROGMORE STEW: NO FROGS WERE HARMED, WE PROMISE.

The dish originated in a small Lowcountry fishing community on St. Helena Island named Frogmore, near Beaufort and Hilton Head. The town was named by John Grayson, and early owner, named after his ancestral English country estate in England. Beaufort historian, Gerhard Spieler believes that the recipe was the invention of local shrimpers who used whatever food items they had on hand to make a stew.

Richard Gay of Gay Seafood Company also claimed to have invented Frogmore Stew. On National Guard duty in Beaufort in the 1960s, he was preparing a cookout of leftovers for his fellow guardsmen, and he brought the recipe home to the community of Frogmore with him, putting out copies of the recipe at his seafood market and selling all the necessary ingredients. Frogmore Stew is also sometimes called Lowcountry boil or Beaufort stew.

A few popular restaurants that serve the Lowcountry boil is Charleston Crab House, Crosby's Fish & Shrimp Company, and The Seafood Pot. Being so close to the water, the shrimp is so fresh. Frogmore Stew is great for feeding a large crowd, so take your friends. It's messy, but so good!

15. FRIED SEAFOOD (WE DEEP FRY ALMOST EVERYTHING!)

Whether it's shrimp, fish or even lobster, you can find an abundance of fried seafood available in South Carolina. A staple in many restaurants is fried catfish. Seasoned and breaded with cornmeal, catfish is flakey, delicious and satisfying. It doesn't take long to cook either. You can find it at places such as The Codfather, Proper Fish & Chips in North Charleston and Luvan's Fish Camp in Conway. Luvan's serves all-you-can eat catfish, so bring your appetite.

16. MEAT 'N THREE

A theory by the late food historian John Egerton, was that the meat 'n three idea is likely an interpretation of old-timey blue-plate specials popular in the early 1900s. Most Meat 'n Three is where you pick the meat entree of your choice, then select three sides. Some meat-and-threes are set up cafeteria-style, where you serve yourself from a buffet. Others offer full table service. Most restaurants that serve this way are family restaurants which have been passed down through generations.

The meats can consist of fried chicken, baked ham, fried fish, meatloaf, and a score of other offerings. The sides can be anything from corn to rice and gravy to butter beans. Missy's, in Florence, is a popular eatery. Another is a chain of restaurants that serves a meat 'n three is Lizard's Thicket. The food is so good that you'll want to lick your plate clean and are sure to leave with your belly stuffed.

Eat Like a Local

17. BLENHEIM GINGER ALE

Blenheim, South Carolina is home to natural springs that are the basis of Blenheim Ginger Ale. The story told is that in 1781, James Spears, a Whig, who was attempting to elude Tory troops. lost his shoe in a water hole. When he came back later to find his lost shoe, he sampled the water and discovered its potent mineral contents.

In the late 1800's, Dr. C. R. May prescribed the water to his patients that had stomachs. The taste wasn't very good, so he added Jamaican Ginger. In 1903, Dr. May and A. J. Matheson started the Blenheim Bottling Company next to the Blenheim Artesian Mineral Springs. The structure which housed the original bottling plant was constructed in 1920 and operated as a working Bottler's Museum for a number of years before tragically burning to the ground in December of 2008. In 1993 the Blenheim Bottling Company was bought by the Schafer Family, who also own the South of the Border Tourist

Complex. Everyone traveling North or South on Interstate 95 knows of South of the Border. You can't miss it! Blenheim Ginger Ale is only sold in glass bottles, keeping it from developing a tin taste. By bottling Blenheim this way, this assures that the ginger ale has the same taste as it did 100 years ago.

18. SWEET POTATOES (AND A SHUT MY MOUTH)

> *"Some people think I look like a sweet potato, I consider myself a spud with a heart of gold."*
>
> ~ Shirley Maclaine

Sweet potatoes are surprisingly in the morning glory family and are distantly related to regular white potatoes. They are also called yams but aren't actually very closely related to yams. It's said that the first Europeans to taste sweet potatoes were

Eat Like a Local

members of Christopher Columbus's expedition in 1492. Later on, explorers found the potatoes under an assortment of local names, but the name which stayed was the indigenous Taino name of batata. The Spanish combined this with the Quechua word for potato, papa, to create the word patata for the common potato. Sweet potatoes have been a part of the diet in the United States for most of its history, especially in the Southeast, mostly due to the warm climate and plentiful rainfall. Sweet potatoes are made into pies, fries, casseroles, and candied. They are fine just by themselves with butter, but some people add cinnamon and brown sugar. Thanksgiving brings the ever-popular sweet potato casseroles. You can find yams or casseroles in many southern cooking restaurants like Cracker Barrel. Cracker Barrel serves up country cooking and can be found up and down the interstates.

19. CHOW CHOW

Chow Chow is a type of pickled relish that is made in a canning jar. It came about in an effort to preserve the abundance of summer produce growing in the backyard, including tomatoes, bell peppers, onions, and more. Chow Chow looks different depending on where the person making it lives and what they grow. Chow Chow is a condiment and can be made spicy or mild. It is served cold.

Just like a lot of old recipes, the origin of chow chow remains somewhat of a debate. Some say that it found its way to the Southern United States during the expulsion of the Acadian people from Nova Scotia to their settlement in Louisiana. This has led some to suggest that the name "chow chow" comes from the French word "chou" for cabbage. Others claim it's connected to the relish of the Chinese rail workers in the 1800s.

In the Northern U.S., it can be found in Pennsylvania Amish communities, and can consist of cauliflower, carrots, beans, onions, bell peppers, etc. In the South, it is made with chopped bell peppers, green tomatoes, sweet onions, and cabbage. There is also a Canadian version that has only green tomatoes and onions in it. Chow chow is a perfect example of making the most of what you have.

20. DUKE'S MAYONNAISE

In 1917, Eugenia Duke began selling sandwiches to the soldiers stationed at Camp Sevier, near her home in Greenville. The sandwiches were a hit, because of her amazing home-made mayonnaise. She sold the sandwiches for a dime each, and Duke made a profit of 2 cents per sandwich. The demand for her mayo becomes so great, that in 1929 she sells the company The C.F. Sauer Company. Eugenia stays on as C.F. Sauer's chief salesperson. Today, Duke's is the 3rd largest mayonnaise brand in the US (behind Hellmann's and Kraft). At first, it was mainly popular in the south, but in 2017 Duke's mayonnaise became available all over the US, New Zealand, Australia, and even the middle east. Southerners swear by the tangy taste of Duke's, and we put it on almost everything. Here, you are judged by what mayo you use. They are not all created the same. To quote my 11-year-old son, Connor, "it just hits different."

21. FRIED CHICKEN

"Everyone loves fried chicken, Don't ever make it. Ever. Buy it from a place that makes good fried chicken."

~ Nora Ephron

Here in South Carolina, we love fried chicken. There's nothing like that juicy, crispy, double-breaded goodness. We learn to cook at a young age in

South Carolina. It's not out of necessity, but we are taught by our mothers and grandmothers. I started cooking at age 15. I remember the first food that I ever made for my now husband was fried chicken. He told me after trying it that he was worried it would be raw, so he was prepared to say it was good just to spare my feelings. After trying it, however, he said it was really delicious and he was astonished at how good of a cook I was at that early age. It's like cooking is ingrained in our DNA here.

Food historians have said that fried chicken is a combination of Scottish cooking methods and African seasoning practices. Fried chicken can be prepared in several ways. It can be deep fried, broasted (breaded and pressure cooked), and pan-fried. If you're in any major city (and some small ones) and you're looking for some really good chicken, you just have to swing by the Chick-Fil-A. We call it the Lord's chicken, because it's heavenly! Some people say that they run on Jesus and Chick-Fil-A. Expect a little wait, because the lines can wrap around the building. However, these restaurants are so efficient and orderly, that you will have chicken in hand in no time. They are so polite here and it's always their pleasure to serve you. Don't go on a Sunday though, because they observe Sundays as holy and are closed.

Chick-fil-A isn't the only chicken place in South Carolina. The number of restaurants is countless. We of course have the usual chains of KFC, Church's, Bojangles, Popeyes, and Zaxby's. We also have Golden Chick. Around Sumter, we have the Chicken Shack. It's a little hole in the wall restaurant that has some really good fried chicken.

If you're looking for something other than fast food chicken, check out Bernie's Restaurant in Columbia. Bernie's has been serving fried chicken for over four decades. Located just up the road from the Gamecocks' stadium, you not only get good fried chicken, but you get fries, a roll, slaw and drink, all under $7.

OJ's Diner in Easley and Greenville is a family-run diner that offers Southern cuisine with a flair. Their food is made from scratch.

In Florence, Sunrise Drive-in is an icon and was once a drive-in many years ago. The fried chicken is prepared to order, so you're sure to get it hot and fresh.

22. HOT SAUCE (WE DO PUT THAT S#&* ON EVERYTHING)

"First you bring the sugar, then you bring the hot sauce."

~ Kevin Ollie

You can't eat anywhere in the country cooking and soul food restaurants in South Carolina without seeing a bottle of hot sauce on the table. Hot sauce is added to greens, beans, and everything in between! If you're into heat, hot sauce created with the Carolina Reaper is not to be missed. Carolina Reaper is a pepper that was certified by Guinness World Records in 2017. The Reaper is a crossbreed of the La Soufriere pepper and the Naga Viper pepper. It is called Carolina, because it was developed in Rock Hill by "Smokin" Ed Currie and reaper because of its shape. It starts out as sweet and immediately feels like you have lava in your mouth. Ed Currie is not only the developer, but has created a business called PuckerButt Pepper Company, which is located in Fort Mill. So, if you can stand the heat, give PuckerButt a try.

23. DESSERTS

Here in the South, we are known for our rich and sinful desserts. There are so many to choose from, but here are a few to get you started and where you can find some of them.

- Benne Wafers - Benne wafers are traditional American cookies originating from Charleston, South Carolina. They are made with a combination of butter, sugar, flour, eggs, baking powder, and benne –

the Bantu word for sesame seeds. In the past, they were a good-luck parting gift for guests at plantation parties. The cookies are crispy and light, with a nice nutty flavor. Nowadays in Charleston, benne wafers are traditionally sold as souvenirs for visitors and locals alike.

- Huguenot Torte - A favorite of Charleston's tearooms, Huguenot torte is a baked apple and pecan or walnut pudding-cake with a crispy meringue-like top, typically served with a dollop of whipped cream. Don't let the name fool you though. It doesn't have French origins nor was it named after the Huguenots, French Protestants who fled to South Carolina in the 17th century for religious freedom. The recipe first showed up in print in a 1950 community cookbook, Charleston Receipts, and was submitted by Evelyn Anderson Florance. She named after the Huguenot Tavern, a restaurant where she worked as a pastry chef.

- Lady Baltimore Cake - This classic is said to have been created toward the end of the 19th century by Florence and Nina Ottelengui who ran

Charleston's Lady Baltimore Tea Room. It wasn't until 1906, when Owen Wister wrote a romance novel by the same name in which he poetically described this luscious dessert, that the cake gained in popularity and has been a Southern favorite ever since. Lady Baltimore is made of several layers of white sponge cake and a rich, marshmallow-like divinity frosting mixed with chopped nuts and dried fruits like raisins, figs, and dates. There is also a version named Lord Baltimore cake which is made with leftover yolks and filled with toasted almonds, crushed macaroons, and candied cherries.

- Coconut Cake – This dessert is made up of several layers of cake with a coconut filling between each layer, all of which is then covered in creamy frosting and more coconut. It's usually made at Christmas and Easter. I remember that my Nana made a coconut cake every year around the holidays. It was her absolute favorite. You can find coconut cake at places all over the state, but Peninsula Grill in Charleston has an amazing twelve-layer cake. It alternates golden coconut milk pound cake with coconut buttercream filling. Each cake is 12 pounds, with 10 sticks of butter and 12 slices. It's definitely a dessert to share or take home for later. Chef Bobby Flay calls this cake his all time favorite, and I have to agree.

- Coca-Cola Cake – Yes, you read that correctly. Coca-Cola Cake first appeared in the 1960s and quickly caught on. This cake combines cola with chocolate, pecans and an incredible frosting. You can't taste the cola, but it gives the cake a very moist texture. You can find this cake at Jestine's in Charleston. You have to at least give it a try.

- Banana Pudding – not an original in the South, but it's been very popular here since the 1900s. There are a few variations, but it's typically made with layering vanilla custard (in my family, we just use store bought vanilla pudding), sliced bananas, and vanilla wafers. As far as the toppings, some people just put another layer of vanilla wafers on top, and others put egg white meringue and toast it. However it's made, it is a popular dessert at any gathering. You can find it at a lot of southern cooking restaurants and definitely at barbeque restaurants.

- Red Velvet Cake - red velvet is everywhere these days. It's not only a delectable cake, but people are even making it in pancake form and cheesecake. This is another dessert that the history is disagreed on. Some say people it originated in New York City, while others believe it was created during the Civil War. That doesn't matter because this cake is so good. It's striking red color, chocolate flavor (from cocoa) and cream cheese frosting is a favorite no matter where you find it. There are so many places in South Carolina to get red velvet. One is Mesha's Sinful Cake & More in Columbia. It's not the traditional cake. Mesha's takes a classic cheesecake recipe and adds chunks of moist red velvet. They top it with a vanilla glaze and whipped cream. This dessert is the best of both worlds.

- Sweet Potato Pie – I know I mentioned this pie back in the sweet potato section, but it bears mentioning again. This is hands down a favorite in South Carolina. Some people even prefer it to

Pumpkin pie. I know in my family; we have always made sweet potato pies at Thanksgiving. Some people put mini marshmallows on top and toast them. I prefer mine without. I usually bake at least two pies every time. One stays home for me (yes, it's mine) and the other I take to my dad, Wendell. He has always made pies for everyone, but in recent years, I have taken up the task and believe me, I do not mind one bit. It's the perfect ending to a Thanksgiving spread when you want something sweet and velvety.

- Crumbl Cookies – while not native to South Carolina, this bakery started in Utah by two cousins. The cookies are made with high quality ingredients and are out of this world. The nearest store to my city is 45 minutes away and honestly, it's worth the drive. Drive 45 minutes for cookies, you say? Yes, I will. They have the usual chocolate chip, but also a rotating variety each week. The first time I tried one, it was the blueberry cheesecake. Soft, buttery sugar cookie topped with cream cheese icing and a blueberry sauce. Let me tell you, I had to sit down. I could only eat half, but this was the best cookie I have ever had in my entire life. If you're looking for phenomenal cookies, they have 32 locations nationwide, with 4 being in South Carolina. Lexington, Summerville, Fort Mill, and Greenville.

24. UPSCALE ESTABLISHMENTS (YES, WE CAN BE FANCY TOO!)

"I think fine dining is dying out everywhere... but I think there will be - and there has to always be - room for at least a small number of really fine, old-school fine-dining restaurants."

~Anthony Bourdain

We can be just as fancy as any other place. South Carolina's beautiful views makes a perfect backdrop for those looking for a "hifalutin" dining experience.

Eat Like a Local

Villa Tronco - Since opening in 1940, Villa Tronco has been a Columbia tradition and is on the list of South Carolina's oldest restaurants, period. Still owned and operated by later generations of the original family, Villa Tronco got its start when Mother Tronco started making Italian food for some northern recruits at Fort Jackson who were homesick for their mother's cooking. The legend has it that Mother Tronco introduced pizza at this restaurant and had to give it away because no one in Columbia knew what it was.

Gaulart & Maliclet (a.k.a. Fast & French) - global cuisine with an emphasis on French. They opened on Broad Street in the Holy City in 1984.

Panini's On The Waterfront - Panini's is located in a building that's seen many rebirths. It was built in 1919 as the Bank of Beaufort but closed in 1926. Since then, it's been a movie theatre, men's clothing store, and at least a couple of restaurants. Panini's serves Italian food.

The Stables at Rose Hill Estate – located in Aiken. The Stables is one of a very few historic working stables in the U.S. that have been successfully converted into a restaurant. Rose Hill Estate was built in 1898. What is now the restaurant was the home of the family's horses.

Millpond Steakhouse – found in Boykin and occupies three historic buildings including an old post office and a general store, both built in the 1800s. All three historic buildings are connected and have a beautiful view of Mill Pond.

Saluda's – Originally built in Columbia by the VFW as an officer's club after the First World War. Saluda's offers Southern cuisine with French and Italian influences.

BONUS TIPS

"Food should be fun."

~ Thomas Keller

Weird Pairings That Just Work

1. Banana and Mayo Sandwich – This sandwich is sweet and tangy. Duke's Mayonnaise, two pieces of bread, and ripe, sliced banana. Some people say eww, but it's pretty good.

2. Tomato Sandwich – Ripe tomato, Duke's Mayonnaise (yes, again), salt and pepper, and two slices of bread.

3. Wendy's Chocolate Frosty and Fries – it's the sweet and savory combo. Who hasn't dipped their fries in their milkshake even once? If you haven't, try it.

4. Sausage Biscuits and Grape Jelly – with this one, even I have never tried it. Once again, it must be the sweet and savory plus the buttery goodness of the biscuit.

5. Butter Beans and Ketchup – This is the only way I eat my butter beans and have done so since I was little. I even like it over rice. What are butter beans, you ask? They go by several names, depending on what part of the country or world you are in. Other names include lima bean, sieva bean, double bean, Madagascar bean, chad bean, or wax bean, and is a legume. I remember shelling butter beans with my Nana (my Grandma Mertie). She grew them in her garden and either canned or froze them. I didn't appreciate them back then as I do now, nor did I appreciate the time spent with her. She's been gone for 19 years now, but I remember sitting with her watching The Price Is Right and shelling beans. Those were simpler times and I miss her every day.

6. Biscuits and Chocolate Gravy – yes, you read that right. It's kind of like putting syrup on biscuits. You put bread in cinnamon and dip in eggs and fry it up to make French toast, so why not chocolate gravy on biscuits?

Eat Like a Local

"Food for the body is not enough. There must be food for the soul."

~ Dorothy Day

"Southern hospitality is not a tangible thing, but an attitude which has been ingrained in southerners forever. It's a feeling of being sincerely welcomed as a guest or a long-lost friend; a way of life that lets people be as warm as the climate. It's an easiness in speaking with total strangers or anyone, a unique friendliness encompassing the whole way of life in the deep south. It's not something one does, it's the way one is."

~ Bee Jackson, Flapper and Queen of the Charleston

Eat Like a Local

The South is the place where the tea is sweet, but accents are sweeter. Summer can start in April and the summers can be sweltering. We consider mac and cheese a vegetable. We are always blessing somebody's heart and we consider Ya'll a proper noun. We like our football and love our momma. If you come here during the fall, you'll no doubt hear about the Carolina/Clemson football rivalry. I'm a Carolina graduate, so I'm partial to them. Besides, no one looks good in orange! Seriously though, if you're thinking of coming to South Carolina, we live up to our State Motto, which is 'Smiling Faces, Beautiful Places." Whether it's snacks, main courses, sides, drinks, or even desserts, our food warms the heart, the soul, and your belly. So, Ya'll come on down and pull up to the table. You're always welcome. If you're not full to bustin', we didn't do our job. To us, that's what hospitality is all about.

RESOURCES:

Wait, there's more info! We're all about abundance in South Carolina, so here are some sites you can go to which may help plan a future trip to our state.

Websites:

South Carolina Travel Magazine
https://www.travelandleisure.com/travel-guide/south-carolina

South Carolina Visitors Guide
https://southcarolinalowcountry.com/

South Carolina Travel Guide
https://www.afar.com/travel-guides/united-states/south-carolina/guide

TravelSC – The Ultimate Sports, Travel & Camping Guide
https://www.travelsc.com/category/united-states/south-carolina/

South Carolina BBQ Trail Map
https://destination-bbq.com/sc-bbq-trail-map/

Apps:

The Green Book of South Carolina
https://greenbookofsc.com/

Traveler of Charleston Mag
https://travelerofcharleston.com/download-the-app/

Eat Like a Local

Taste of the Seasons

South Carolina State Farmers Market
> Columbia

Watsonia Farms
> Monetta

Dorr Farms
> Gable

Mcleod Farms
> MacBee

Carolina Vineyards Winery
> Myrtle Beach

READ OTHER BOOKS BY CZYK PUBLISHING

Eat Like a Local United States Cities & Towns

Eat Like a Local United States

Eat Like a Local- Oklahoma: Oklahoma Food Guide

Eat Like a Local- North Carolina: North Carolina Food Guide

Eat Like a Local- New York City: New York City Food Guide

Children's Book: Charlie the Cavalier Travels the World by Lisa Rusczyk

Eat Like a Local

Follow *Eat Like a Local* on Amazon.
Join our mailing list for new books

http://bit.ly/EatLikeaLocalbooks

CZYKPublishing.com

Printed in Great Britain
by Amazon